Beethoven's Beautiful Melodies

Arranged by David Pearl

CONTENTS

ISBN-13: 978-1-57560-932-4
ISBN-10: 1-57560-932-0

Cherry Lane Music Company
Director of Publications/Project Editor: Mark Phillips
Manager of Publications: Gabrielle Fastman

Visit our website at www.cherrylane.com

Adelaide

By Ludwig van Beethoven

Moderately slow

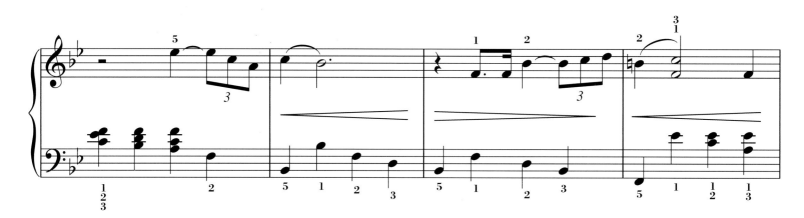

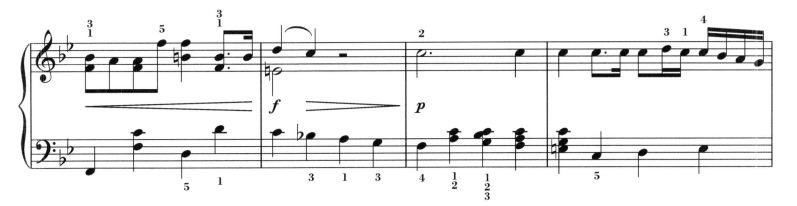

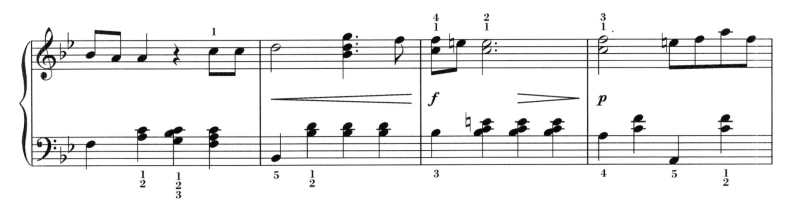

3

Allegro in G for Mechanical Clock

By Ludwig van Beethoven

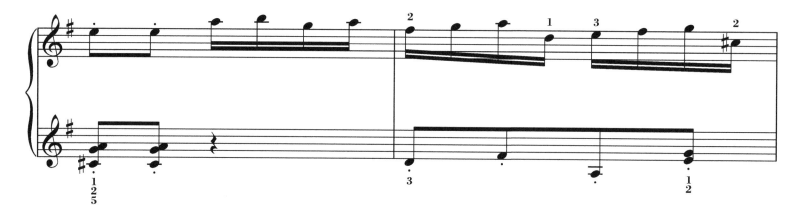

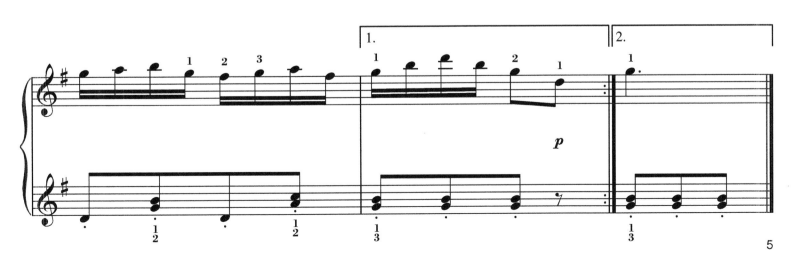

5

Egmont Overture

By Ludwig van Beethoven

Moderately fast

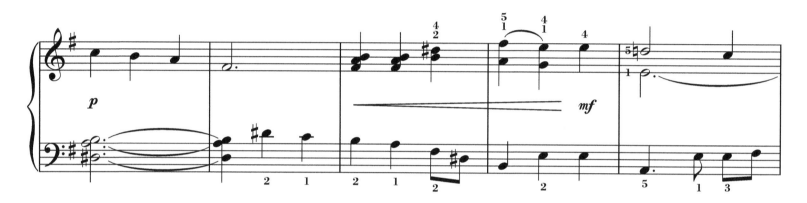

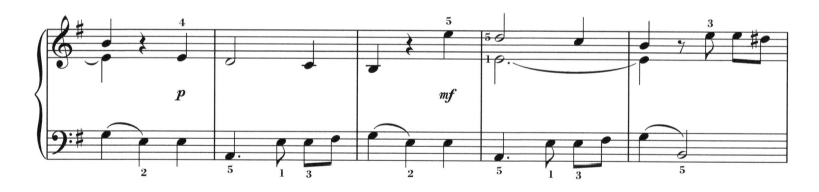

cresc.

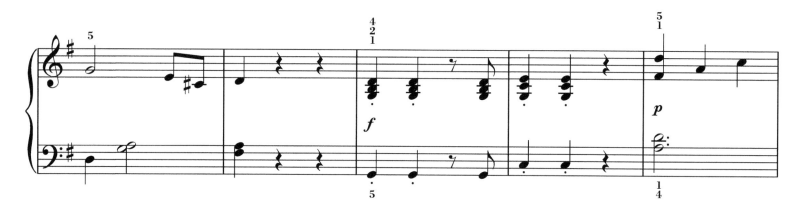

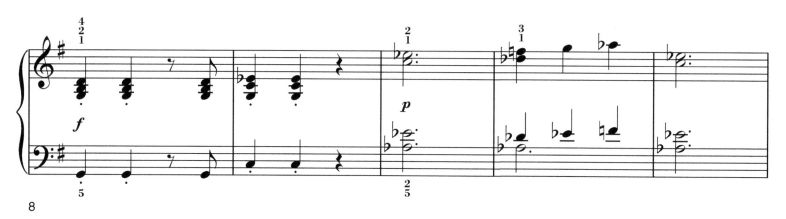

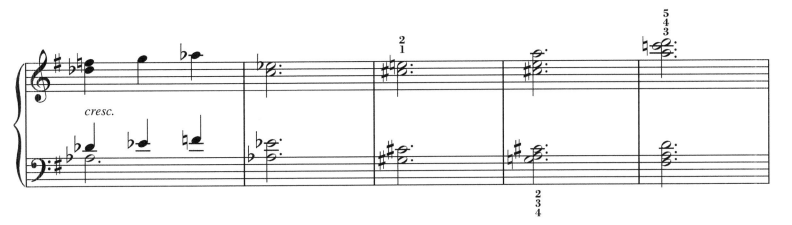

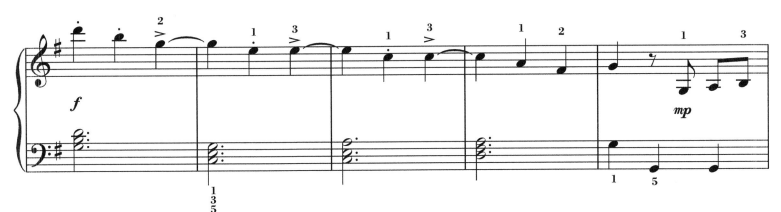

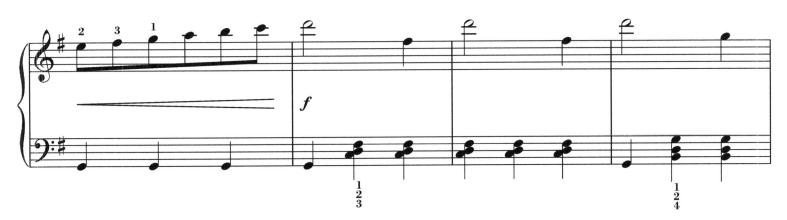

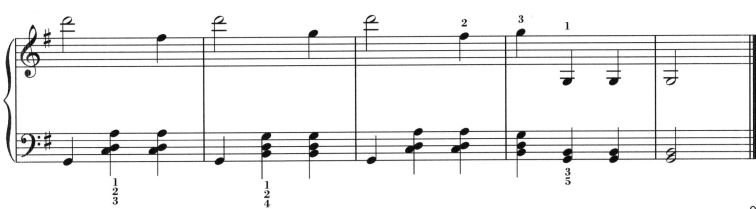

Für Elise

By Ludwig van Beethoven

Moderately

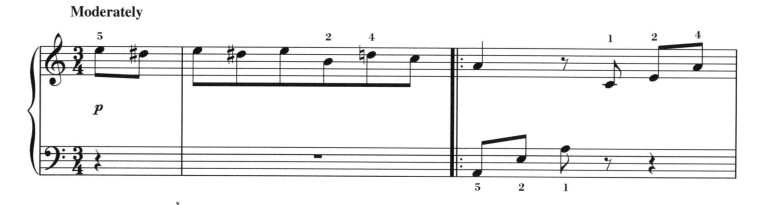

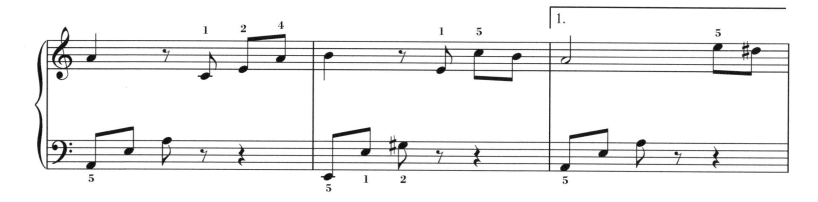

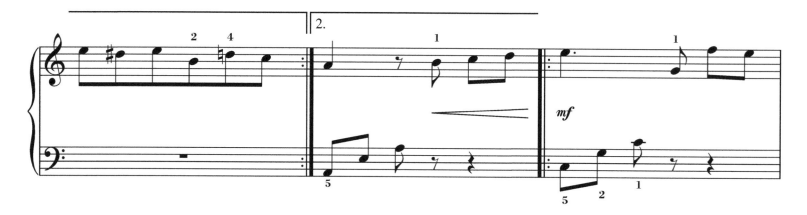

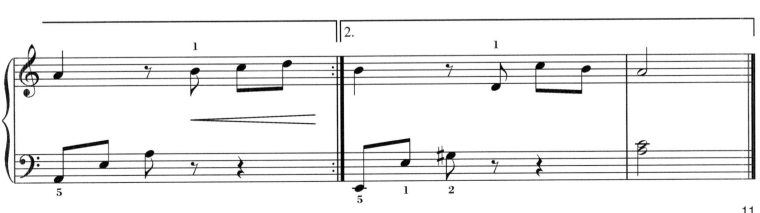

Minuet in G

By Ludwig van Beethoven

Moderately

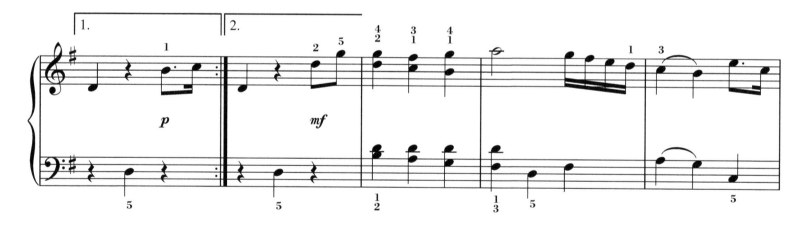

Piano Concerto No. 3

Third Movement

By Ludwig van Beethoven

Moderately fast

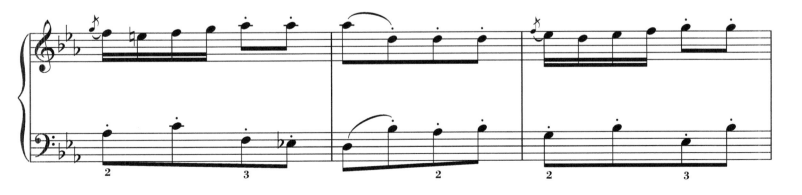

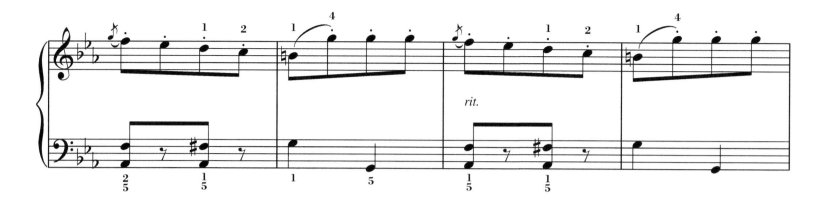

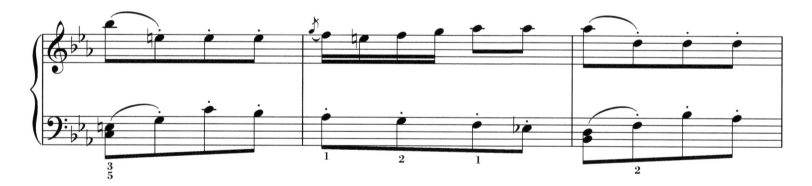

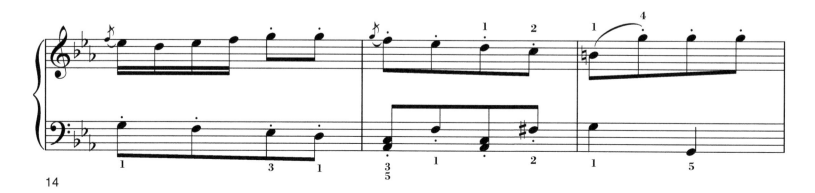

14

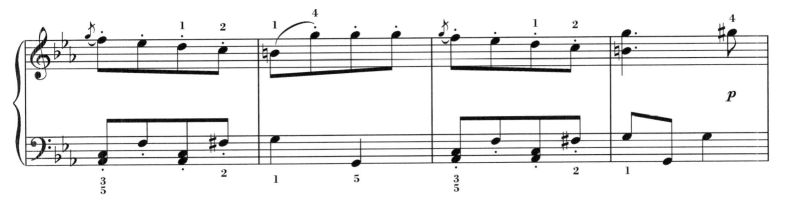

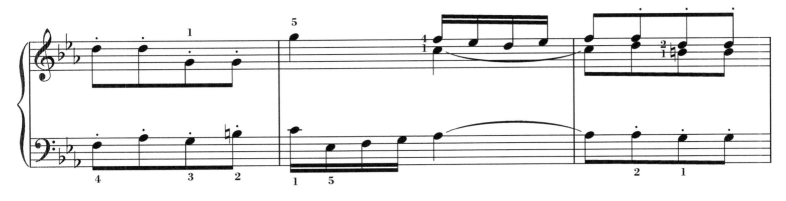

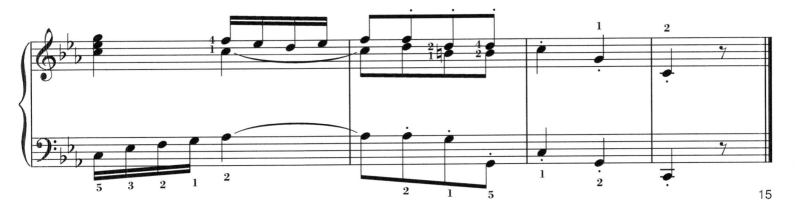

15

Piano Concerto No. 5

Second Movement

By Ludwig van Beethoven

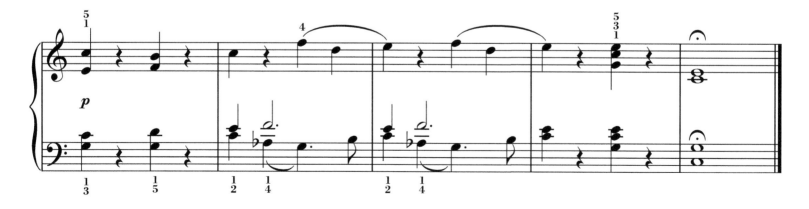

Piano Sonata No. 8 "Pathetique"

Second Movement

By Ludwig van Beethoven

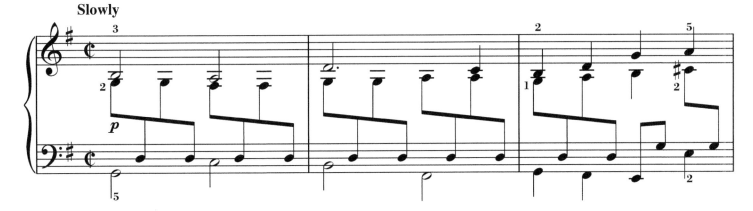

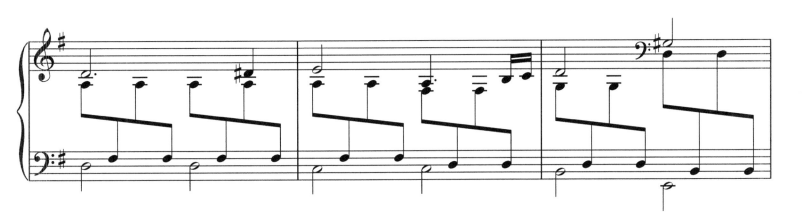

Piano Sonata No. 14 "Moonlight"

First Movement

By Ludwig van Beethoven

Slowly, delicately

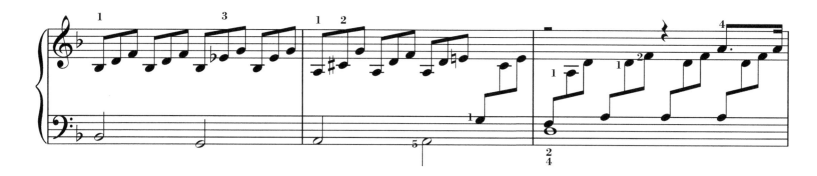

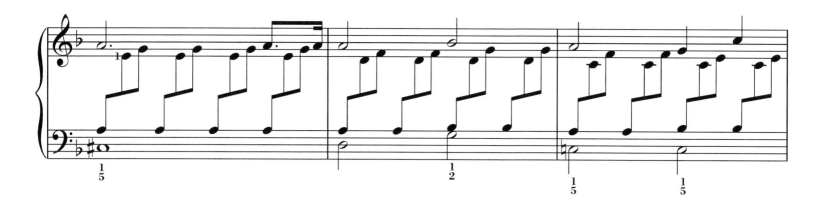

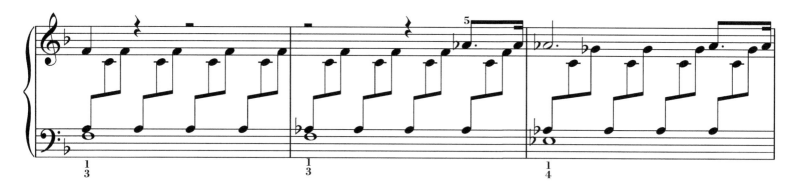

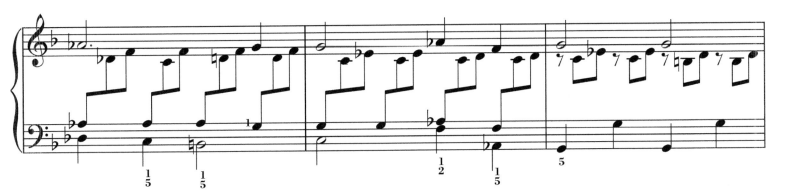

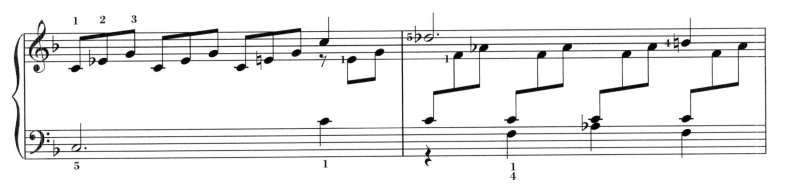

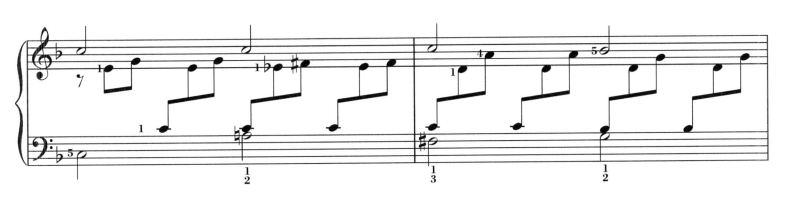

19

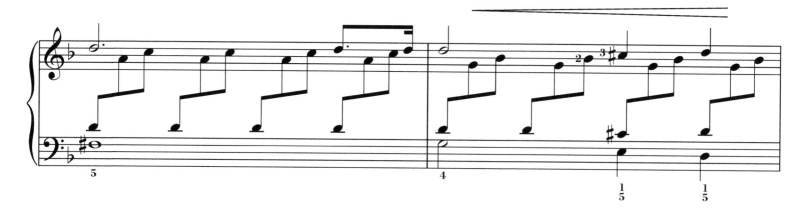

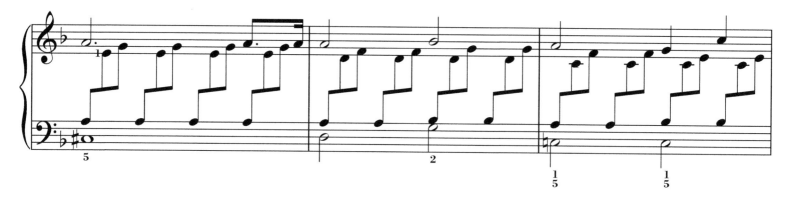

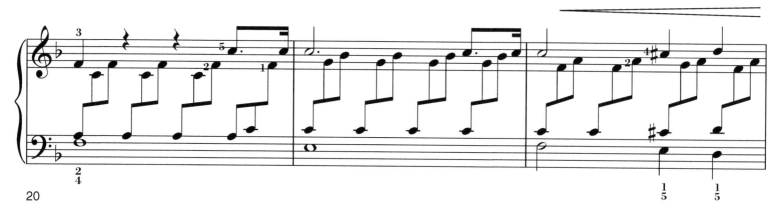

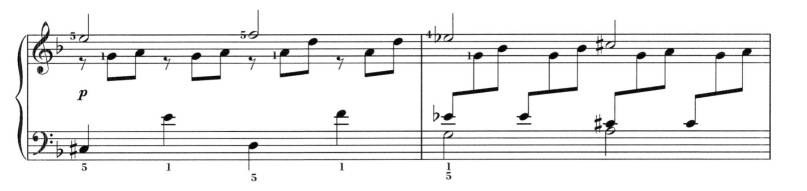

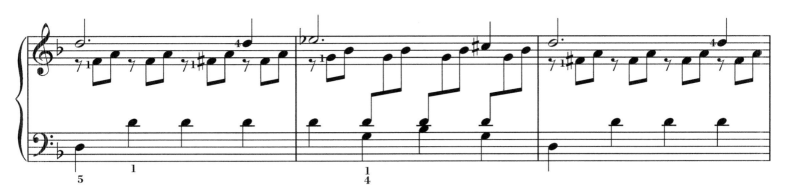

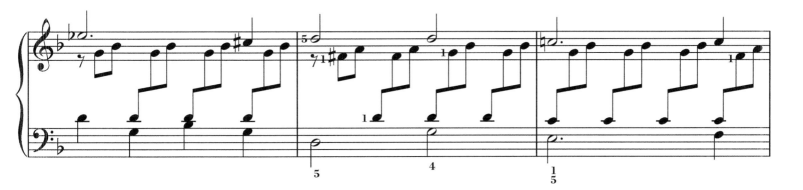

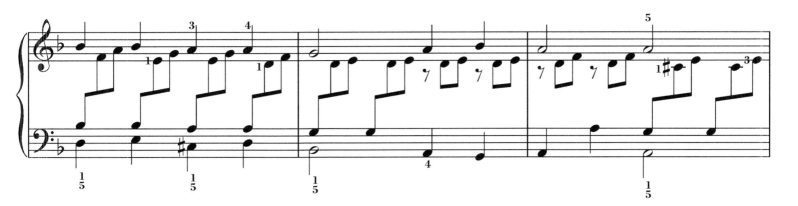

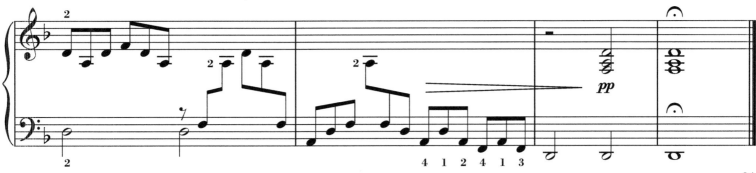

21

Piano Sonata No. 19

First Movement

By Ludwig van Beethoven

Moderately slow

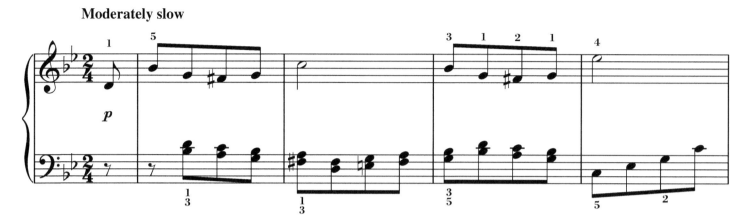

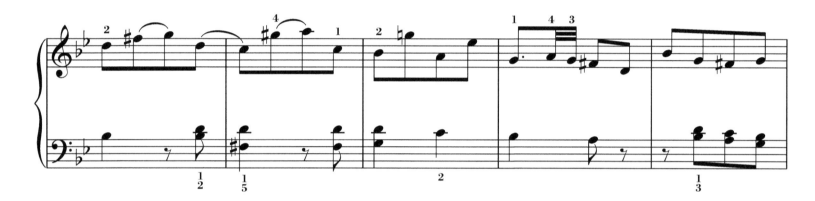

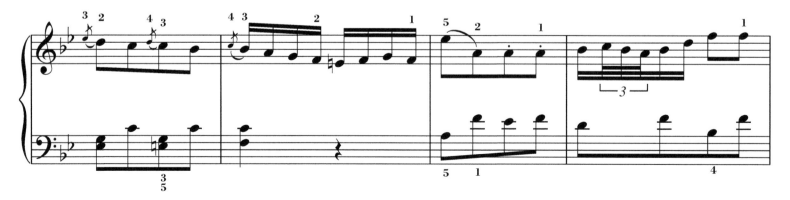

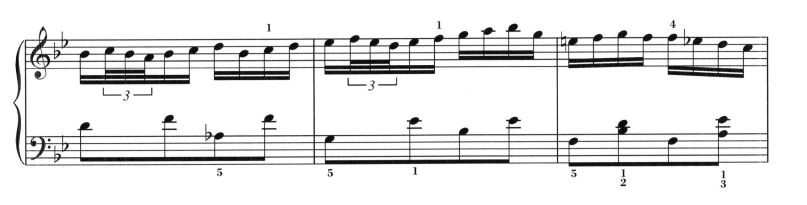

Piano Sonata No. 30

Third Movement

By Ludwig van Beethoven

Very slowly

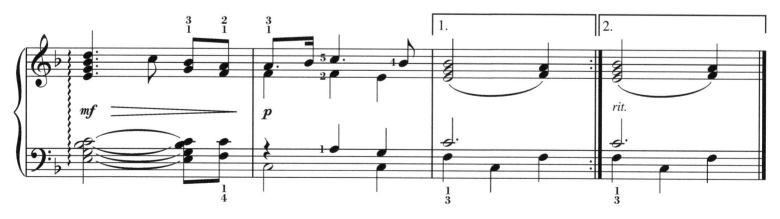

Piano Sonata No. 31

First Movement

By Ludwig van Beethoven

Moderately

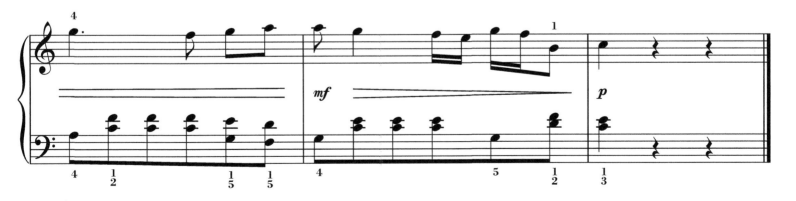

Piano Trio No. 7 "Archduke"

Third Movement

By Ludwig van Beethoven

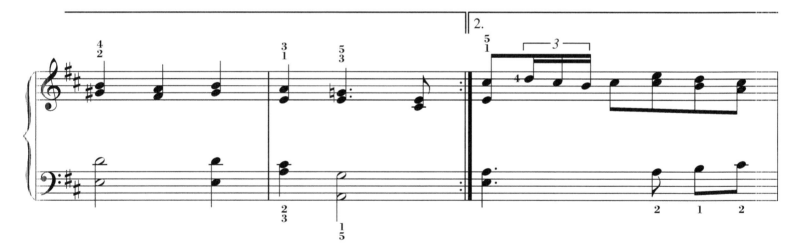

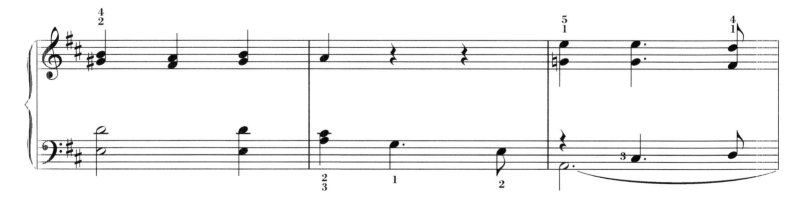

Quintet for Piano and Winds

Second Movement

By Ludwig van Beethoven

Moderately slow

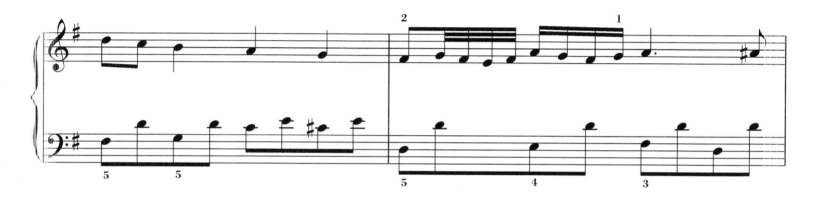

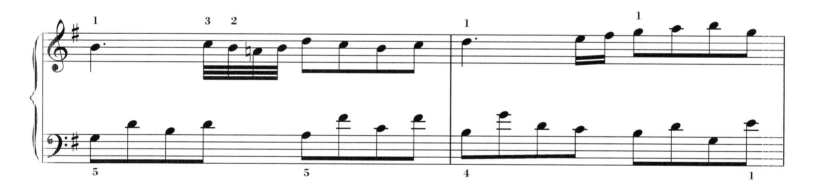

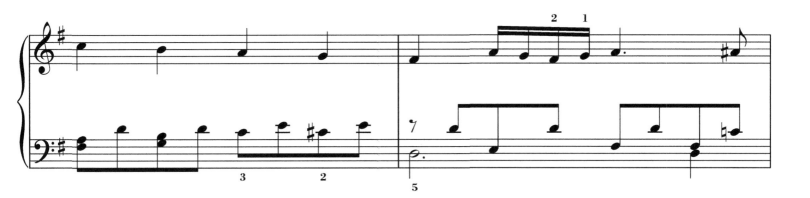

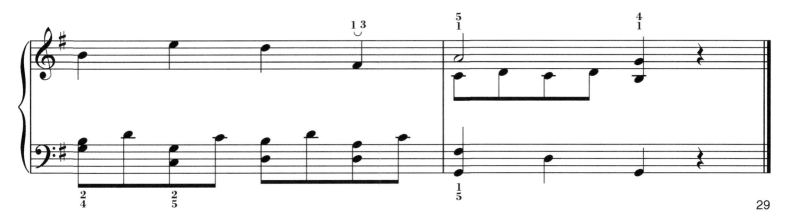

Romance No. 2

for Violin and Orchestra

By Ludwig van Beethoven

Very slowly

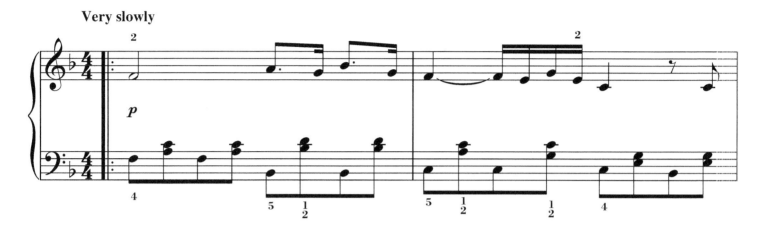

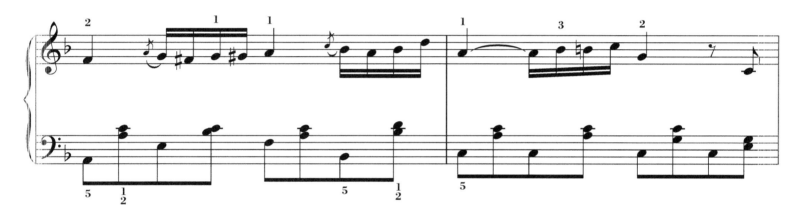

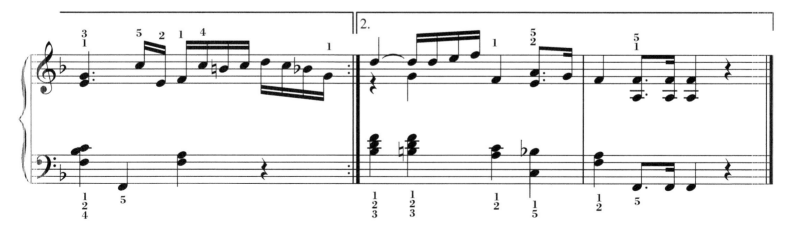

Symphony No. 1

Second Movement

By Ludwig van Beethoven

Moderately

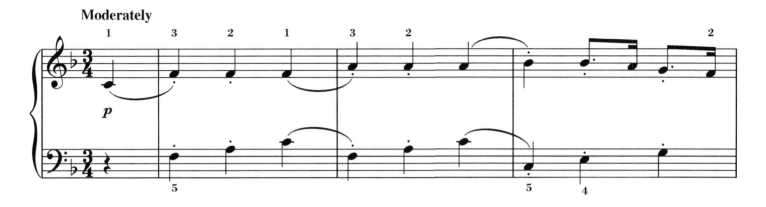

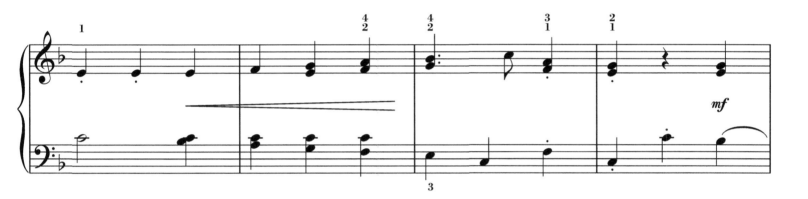

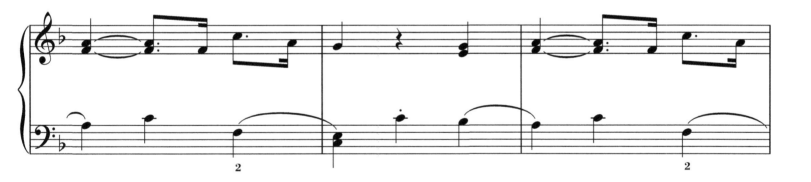

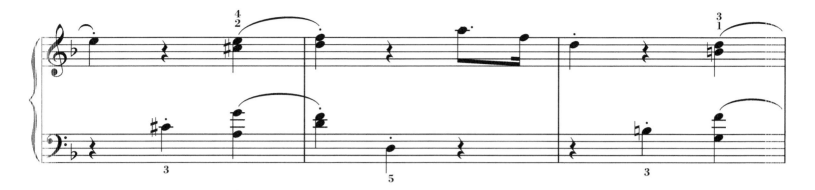

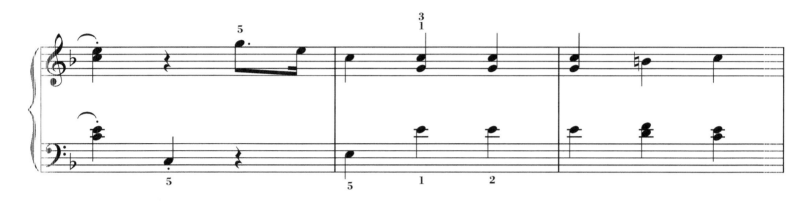

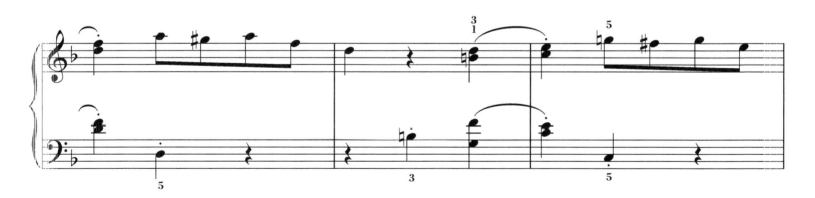

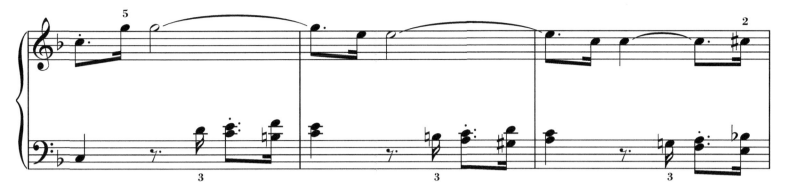

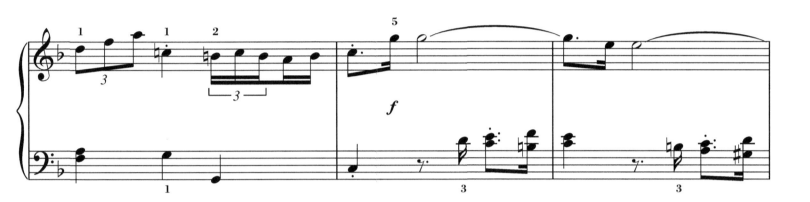

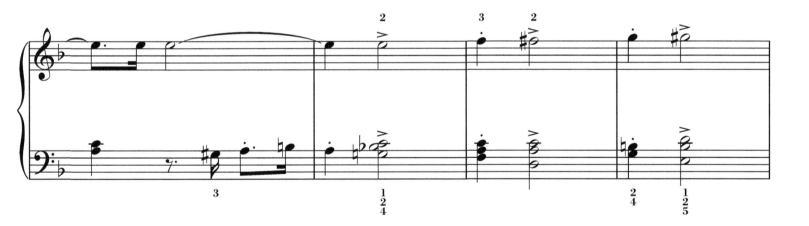

Sonatina

By Ludwig van Beethoven

Moderately

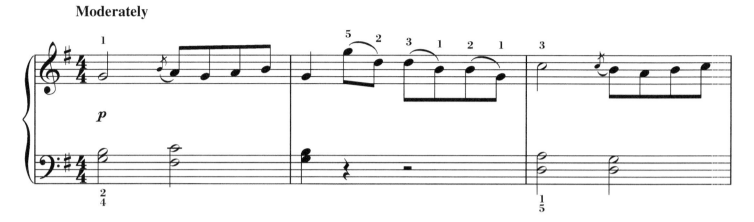

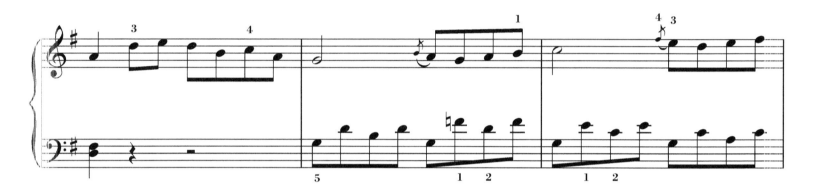

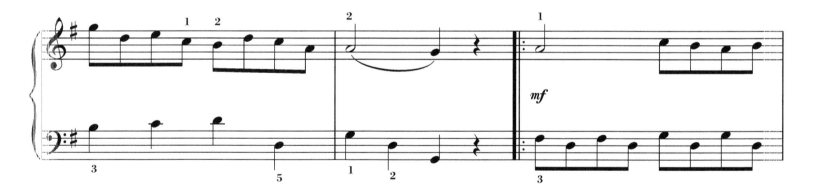

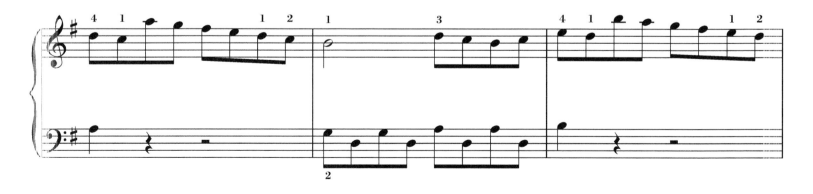

String Quartet No. 10 "Harp"

Second Movement

By Ludwig van Beethoven

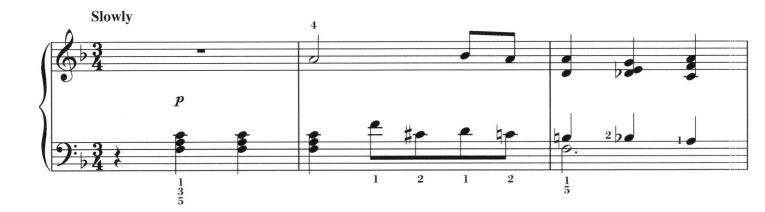

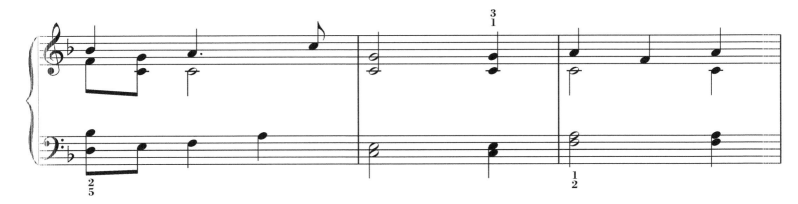

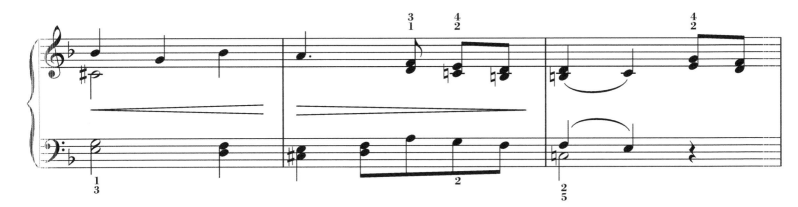

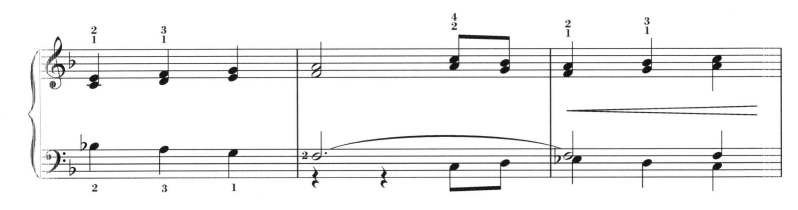

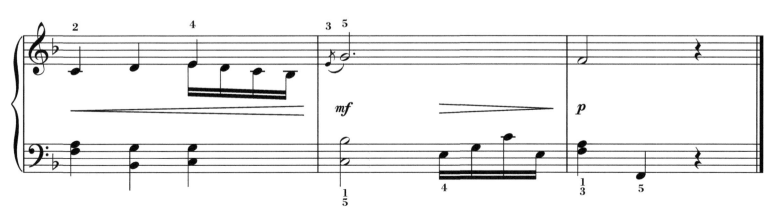

String Quartet No. 13

Fifth Movement ("Cavatina")

By Ludwig van Beethoven

Very slow, expressively

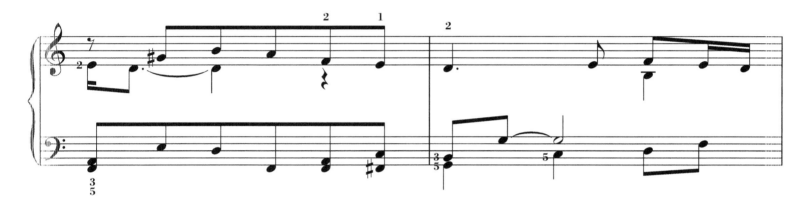

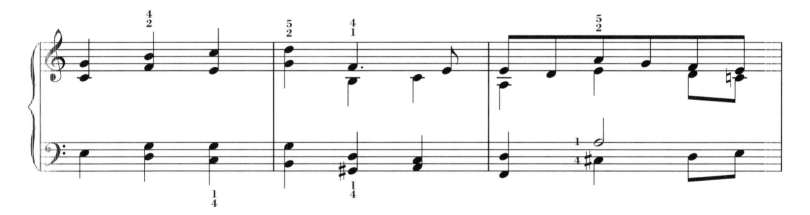

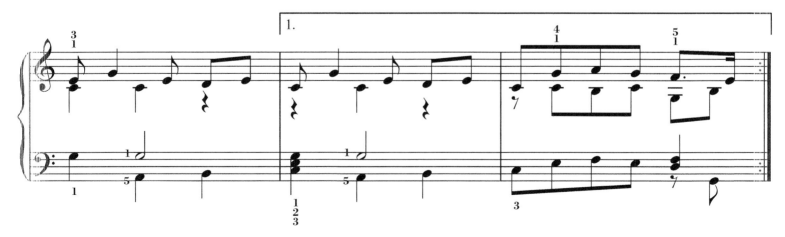

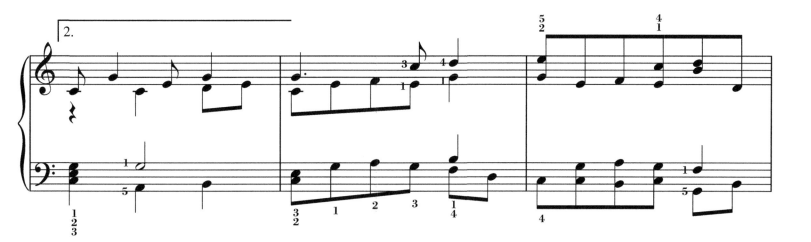

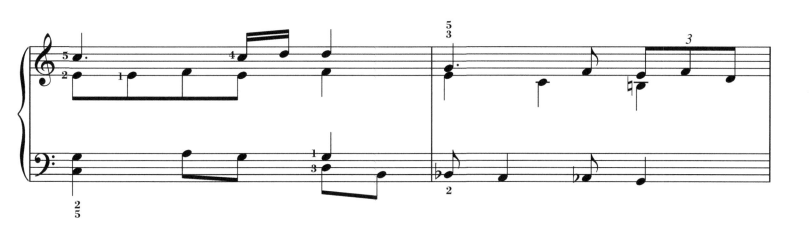

Symphony No. 6 "Pastoral"

First Movement

By Ludwig van Beethoven

Moderately

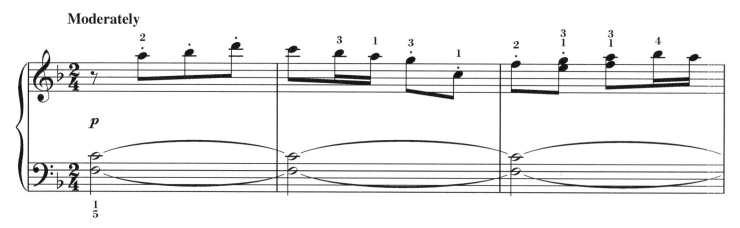

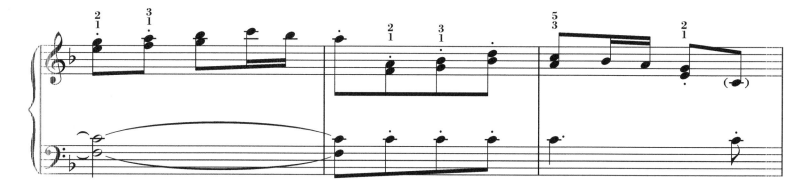

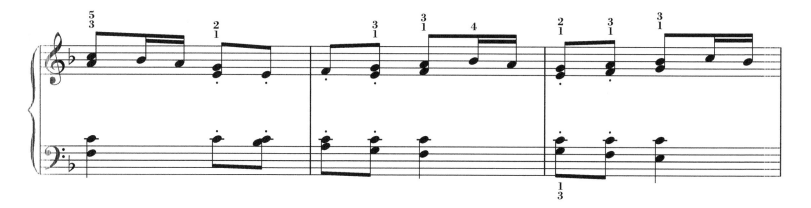

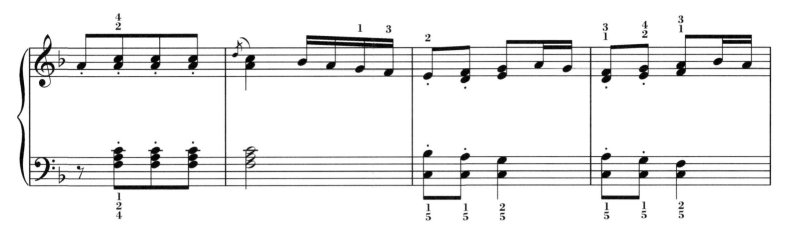

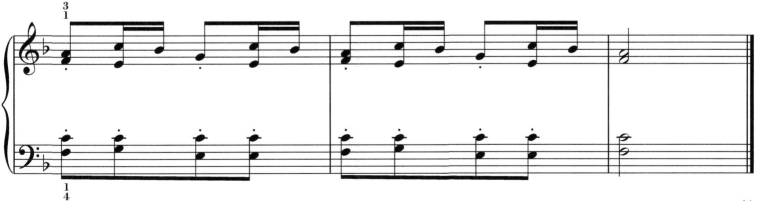

Symphony No. 9

Fourth Movement ("Ode to Joy")

By Ludwig van Beethoven

Moderately fast

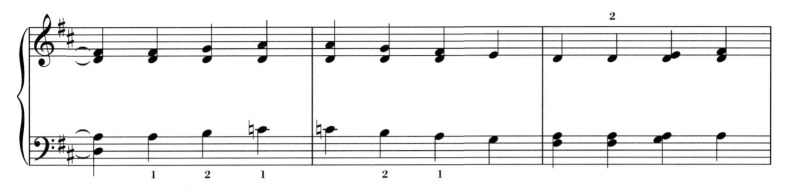

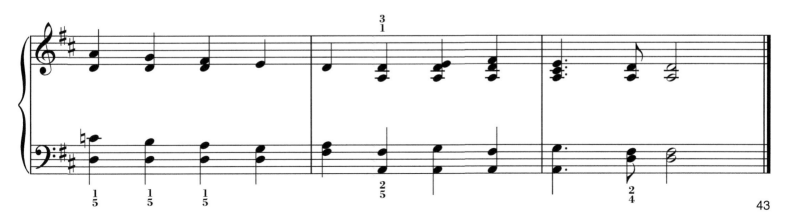

Violin Sonata No. 9 "Kreutzer"

Second Movement

By Ludwig van Beethoven

Slowly

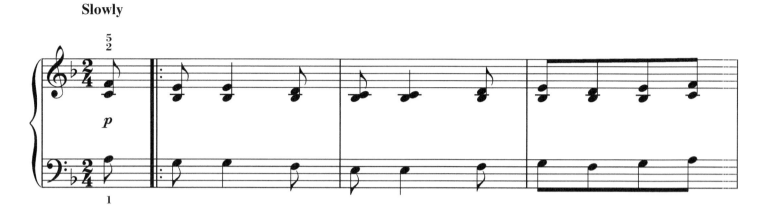

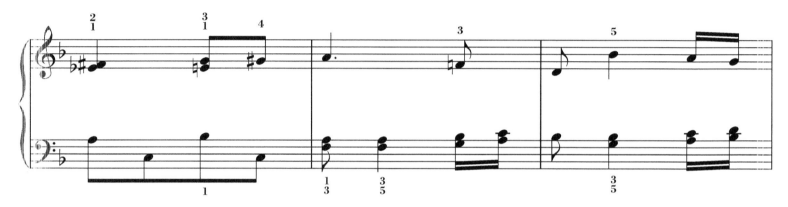

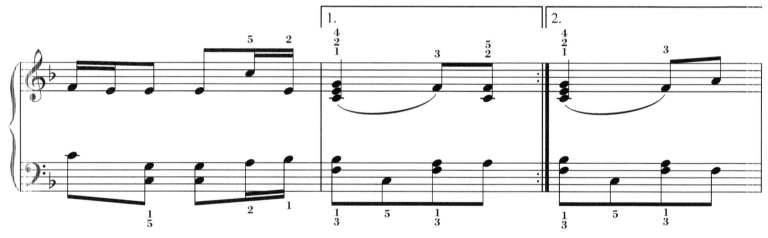

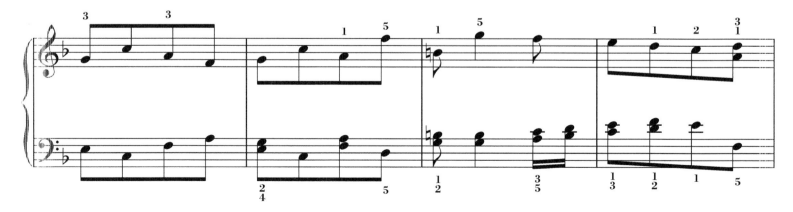

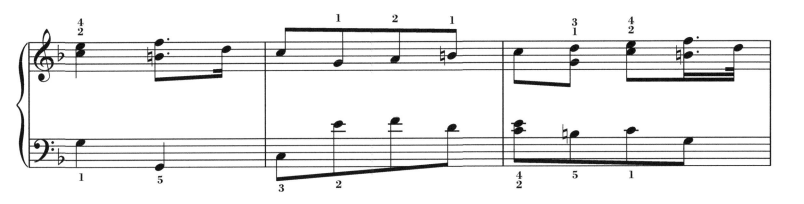

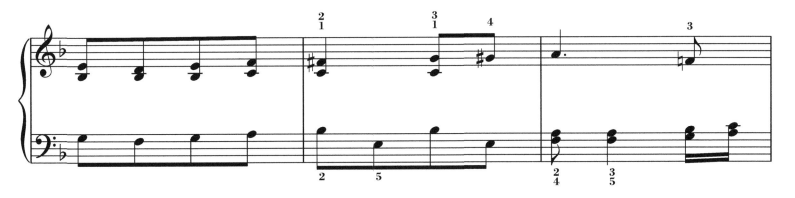

Symphony No. 2

Second Movement

By Ludwig van Beethoven

THE MOST REQUESTED SERIES

ACOUSTIC SONGS

48 songs: American Pie • Black Water • The Boxer • Cat's in the Cradle • Crazy Little Thing Called Love • Free Fallin' • Friend of the Devil • I Walk the Line • Landslide • More Than Words • Patience • Redemption Song • Summer Breeze • Toes • Wish You Were Here • and many more.

00001518 Piano/Vocal/Guitar $19.99

BOSSA NOVA & SAMBA SONGS

61 songs: Bonita • Don't Ever Go Away (Por Causa De Voce) • A Felicidade • The Girl from Ipanema (Garôta De Ipanema) • How Insensitive (Insensatez) • The Look of Love • Mas Que Nada • So Nice (Summer Samba) • Triste • and many more.

00154900 Piano/Vocal/Guitar.......................$24.99

CHILDREN'S SONGS

73 songs: Addams Family Theme • Be Our Guest • Edelweiss • Ghostbusters • Happy Birthday to You • Linus and Lucy • Put on a Happy Face • Sing • So Long, Farewell • Take Me Out to the Ball Game • This Land Is Your Land • You Are My Sunshine • and many more.

00145525 Piano/Vocal/Guitar.......................$19.99

CHRISTMAS SONGS

69 songs: Blue Christmas • Christmas Time Is Here • Deck the Hall • Feliz Navidad • Grandma Got Run over by a Reindeer • I'll Be Home for Christmas • Jingle Bells • Little Saint Nick • Nuttin' for Christmas • Rudolph the Red-Nosed Reindeer • Silent Night • and more.

00001563 Piano/Vocal/Guitar....................... $24.99

CLASSIC ROCK SONGS

60 songs: Africa • Bang a Gong (Get It On) • Don't Stop Believin' • Feelin' Alright • Hello, It's Me • Layla • Life in the Fast Lane • Maybe I'm Amazed • Money • Only the Good Die Young • Small Town • Tiny Dancer • We Are the Champions • and more!

02501632 Piano/Vocal/Guitar....................... $24.99

COUNTRY SONGS

47 songs: Cruise • Don't You Wanna Stay • Fly Over States • Gunpowder & Lead • How Do You Like Me Now?! • If I Die Young • Need You Now • Red Solo Cup • The Thunder Rolls • Wide Open Spaces • and more.

00127660 Piano/Vocal/Guitar.......................$19.99

COUNTRY LOVE SONGS

59 songs: Always on My Mind • Amazed • Crazy • Forever and Ever, Amen • I Will Always Love You • Love Story • Stand by Your Man • Through the Years • When You Say Nothing at All • You're Still the One • and more.

00159649 Piano/Vocal/Guitar.......................$29.99

FOLK/POP SONGS

62 songs: Blowin' in the Wind • Do You Believe in Magic • Fast Car • The House of the Rising Sun • If I Were a Carpenter • Leaving on a Jet Plane • Morning Has Broken • The Night They Drove Old Dixie Down • Puff the Magic Dragon • The Sound of Silence • Teach Your Children • and more.

00110225 Piano/Vocal/Guitar $22.99

ISLAND SONGS

60 songs: Beyond the Sea • Blue Hawaii • Coconut • Don't Worry, Be Happy • Electric Avenue • Escape (The Pina Colada Song) • I Can See Clearly Now • Island Girl • Kokomo • Redemption Song • Surfer Girl • Tiny Bubbles • and many more.

00197925 Piano/Vocal/Guitar $19.99

JAZZ STANDARDS

75 songs: All the Things You Are • Blue Skies • Embraceable You • Fascinating Rhythm • God Bless' the Child • I Got Rhythm • Mood Indigo • Pennies from Heaven • Satin Doll • Stella by Starlight • Summertime • The Very Thought of You • and more.

00102988 Piano/Vocal/Guitar.......................$19.99

MOVIE SONGS

73 songs: Born Free • Chariots of Fire • Endless Love • I Will Always Love You • James Bond Theme • Mrs. Robinson • Moon River • Over the Rainbow • Stand by Me • Star Wars (Main Theme) • (I've Had) the Time of My Life • The Wind Beneath My Wings • and more!

00102882 Piano/Vocal/Guitar.......................$19.99

POP/FOLK SONGS

60 songs: Alison • Annie's Song • Both Sides Now • The Boxer • California Girls • Fire and Rain • Joy to the World • Longer • Son-Of-A-Preacher Man • Summer in the City • Up on the Roof • and many more.

00145529 Piano/Vocal/Guitar.......................$22.99

SONGS OF THE '60s

72 songs: Aquarius • The Beat Goes On • Beyond the Sea • Happy Together • Hey Jude • King of the Road • Like a Rolling Stone • Save the Last Dance for Me • Son-Of-A-Preacher Man • These Eyes • Under the Boardwalk • Up on the Roof • and more.

00110207 Piano/Vocal/Guitar $24.99

SONGS OF THE '70s

58 songs: Bohemian Rhapsody • Desperado • Hello, It's Me • I Will Survive • Just the Way You Are • Let It Be • Night Moves • Rocky Mountain High • Summer Breeze • Time in a Bottle • You're So Vain • Your Song • and many more.

00119714 Piano/Vocal/Guitar $24.99

SONGS OF THE '80s

59 songs: Africa • Billie Jean • Come on Eileen • Every Breath You Take • Faith • Footloose • Hello • Here I Go Again • Jessie's Girl • Like a Virgin • Livin' on a Prayer • Open Arms • Rosanna • Sweet Child O' Mine • Take on Me • Uptown Girl • and more.

00111668 Piano/Vocal/Guitar $27.99

SONGS OF THE '90s

51 songs: All I Wanna Do • ...Baby One More Time • Barely Breathing • Creep • Fields of Gold • From a Distance • Livin' La Vida Loca • Losing My Religion • Semi-Charmed Life • Smells like Teen Spirit • 3 AM • Under the Bridge • Who Will Save Your Soul • You Oughta Know • and more.

00111971 Piano/Vocal/Guitar.........................$19.99

WEDDING RECEPTION SONGS

54 songs: Celebration • How Sweet It Is (To Be Loved by You) • Hungry Eyes • I Will Always Love You • In My Life • Isn't She Lovely • Last Dance • Let's Get It On • Love and Marriage • My Girl • Sunrise, Sunset • Unforgettable • The Way You Look Tonight • and more.

02501750 Piano/Vocal/Guitar.......................$19.99

HAL•LEONARD®

www.halleonard.com
Prices, content, and availability subject to change without notice.

0422
080

More Big-Note & Easy Piano Books

For a complete listing of Cherry Lane titles available, including contents listings, please visit our web site at www.cherrylaneprint.com

BEAUTIFUL POP BALLADS FOR EASY PIANO
31 lovely pop songs in simplified arrangements, including: Don't Know Why • From a Distance • Hero • Just Once • My Cherie Amour • November Rain • Open Arms • Time After Time • Unchained Melody • What a Wonderful World • Your Song • and more.
_____ 02502450 Easy Piano $12.99

CHOPIN FOR EASY PIANO
This special easy piano version features the composer's intricate melodies, harmonies and rhythms newly arranged so that virtually all pianists can experience the thrill of playing Chopin at the piano! Includes 20 favorites mazurkas, nocturnes, polonaises, preludes and waltzes.
_____ 02501483 Easy Piano $7.99

CLASSICAL CHRISTMAS
Easy solo arrangements of 30 wonderful holiday songs: Ave Maria • Dance of the Sugar Plum Fairy • Evening Prayer • Gesu Bambino • Hallelujah! • He Shall Feed His Flock • March of the Toys • O Come, All Ye Faithful • O Holy Night • Pastoral Symphony • Sheep May Safely Graze • Sinfonia • Waltz of the Flowers • and more.
_____ 02500112 Easy Piano Solo $9.95

BEST OF JOHN DENVER
A collection of 18 Denver classics, including: Leaving on a Jet Plane • Take Me Home, Country Roads • Rocky Mountain High • Follow Me • and more.
_____ 02505512 Easy Piano $9.95

JOHN DENVER ANTHOLOGY
Easy arrangements of 34 of the finest from this beloved artist. Includes: Annie's Song • Fly Away • Follow Me • Grandma's Feather Bed • Leaving on a Jet Plane • Perhaps Love • Rocky Mountain High • Sunshine on My Shoulders • Take Me Home, Country Roads • Thank God I'm a Country Boy • and many more.
_____ 02501366 Easy Piano $19.99

EASY BROADWAY SHOWSTOPPERS
Easy piano arrangements of 16 traditional and new Broadway standards, including: "Impossible Dream" from Man of La Mancha • "Unusual Way" from Nine • "This Is the Moment" from Jekyll & Hyde • many more.
_____ 02505517 Easy Piano $12.95

A FAMILY CHRISTMAS AROUND THE PIANO
25 songs for hours of family fun, including: Away in a Manger • Deck the Hall • The First Noel • God Rest Ye Merry, Gentlemen • Hark! the Herald Angels Sing • Jingle Bells • Jolly Old St. Nicholas • Joy to the World • O Little Town of Bethlehem • Silent Night, Holy Night • The Twelve Days of Christmas • and more.
_____ 02500398 Easy Piano $8.99

FAVORITE CELTIC SONGS FOR EASY PIANO
Easy arrangements of 40 Celtic classics, including: The Ash Grove • The Bluebells of Scotland • A Bunch of Thyme • Danny Boy • Finnegan's Wake • I'll Tell Me Ma • Loch Lomond • My Wild Irish Rose • The Rose of Tralee • and more!
_____ 02501306 Easy Piano $12.99

HOLY CHRISTMAS CAROLS COLORING BOOK
A terrific songbook with 7 sacred carols and lots of coloring pages for the young pianist. Songs include: Angels We Have Heard on High • The First Noel • Hark! The Herald Angels Sing • It Came upon a Midnight Clear • O Come All Ye Faithful • O Little Town of Bethlehem • Silent Night.
_____ 02500277 Five-Finger Piano $6.95

JEKYLL & HYDE – VOCAL SELECTIONS
Ten songs from the Wildhorn/Bricusse Broadway smash, arranged for big-note: In His Eyes • It's a Dangerous Game • Lost in the Darkness • A New Life • No One Knows Who I Am • Once Upon a Dream • Someone Like You • Sympathy, Tenderness • Take Me as I Am • This Is the Moment.
_____ 02500023 Big-Note Piano $9.95

JACK JOHNSON ANTHOLOGY
Easy arrangements of 27 of the best from this Hawaiian singer/songwriter, including: Better Together • Breakdown • Flake • Fortunate Fool • Good People • Sitting, Waiting, Wishing • Taylor • and more.
_____ 02501313 Easy Piano $19.99

JUST FOR KIDS – NOT! CHRISTMAS SONGS
This unique collection of 14 Christmas favorites is fun for the whole family! Kids can play the full-sounding big-note solos alone, or with their parents (or teachers) playing accompaniment for the thrill of four-hand piano! Includes: Deck the Halls • Jingle Bells • Silent Night • What Child Is This? • and more.
_____ 02505510 Big-Note Piano $8.95

JUST FOR KIDS – NOT! CLASSICS
Features big-note arrangements of classical masterpieces, plus optional accompaniment for adults. Songs: Air on the G String • Dance of the Sugar Plum Fairy • Für Elise • Jesu, Joy of Man's Desiring • Ode to Joy • Pomp and Circumstance • The Sorcerer's Apprentice • William Tell Overture • and more!
_____ 02505513 Classics $7.95
_____ 02500301 More Classics $8.95

JUST FOR KIDS – NOT! FUN SONGS
Fun favorites for kids everywhere in big-note arrangements for piano, including: Bingo • Eensy Weensy Spider • Farmer in the Dell • Jingle Bells • London Bridge • Pop Goes the Weasel • Puff the Magic Dragon • Skip to My Lou • Twinkle, Twinkle Little Star • and more!
_____ 02505523 Fun Songs $7.95

JUST FOR KIDS – NOT! TV THEMES & MOVIE SONGS
Entice the kids to the piano with this delightful collection of songs and themes from movies and TV. These big-note arrangements include themes from The Brady Bunch and The Addams Family, as well as Do-Re-Mi (The Sound of Music), theme from Beetlejuice (Day-O) and Puff the Magic Dragon. Each song includes an accompaniment part for teacher or adult so that the kids can experience the joy of four-hand playing as well! Plus performance tips.
_____ 02505507 TV Themes & Movie Songs $9.95
_____ 02500304 More TV Themes & Movie Songs $9.95

BEST OF JOHN MAYER FOR EASY PIANO
15 of Mayer's best arranged for easy piano, including: Daughters • Gravity • My Stupid Mouth • No Such Thing • Waiting on the World to Change • Who Says • Why Georgia • Your Body Is a Wonderland • and more.
_____ 02501705 Easy Piano $16.99

POKEMON 2 B.A. MASTER
This great songbook features easy piano arrangements of 13 tunes from the hit TV series: 2.B.A. Master • Double Trouble (Team Rocket) • Everything Changes • Misty's Song • My Best Friends • Pokémon (Dance Mix) • Pokémon Theme • PokéRAP • The Time Has Come (Pikachu's Goodbye) • Together, Forever • Viridian City • What Kind of Pokémon Are You? • You Can Do It (If You Really Try). Includes a full-color, 8-page pull-out section featuring characters and scenes from this super hot show.
_____ 02500145 Easy Piano $12.95

POPULAR CHRISTMAS CAROLS COLORING BOOK
Kids are sure to love this fun holiday songbook! It features five-finger piano arrangements of seven Christmas classics, complete with coloring pages throughout! Songs include: Deck the Hall • Good King Wenceslas • Jingle Bells • Jolly Old St. Nicholas • O Christmas Tree • Up on the Housetop • We Wish You a Merry Christmas.
_____ 02500276 Five-Finger Piano $6.95

PUFF THE MAGIC DRAGON & 54 OTHER ALL-TIME CHILDREN'S FAVORITESONGS
55 timeless songs enjoyed by generations of kids, and sure to be favorites for years to come. Songs include: A-Tisket A-Tasket • Alouette • Eensy Weensy Spider • The Farmer in the Dell • I've Been Working on the Railroad • If You're Happy and You Know It • Joy to the World • Michael Finnegan • Oh Where, Oh Where Has My Little Dog Gone • Silent Night • Skip to My Lou • This Old Man • and many more.
_____ 02500017 Big-Note Piano $12.95

See your local music dealer or contact:

🍒 cherry lane music company

EXCLUSIVELY DISTRIBUTED BY
HAL•LEONARD®
7777 W. BLUEMOUND RD. P.O. BOX 13819 MILWAUKEE, WI 53213

Prices, contents, and availability subject to change without notice.

1112